"Phil" osophy by Phil Dunphy

Re-created by Rachel Paniccia

D1362131

Always look people in the eye. Even if they're blind. Just say, "I'm looking you in the eye."

Phil Dunphy

If you get pulled over for speeding, tell the policeman your spouse has diarrhea.

Phil Dunphy

You only get one chance at a first impression. I suggest Julie Child, because it's easy to do. "Save the giblets!"

Phil Dunphy

Dance until your feet hurt. Sing until your lungs hurt. Act until you're William Hurt.

Phil Dunphy

Take a lesson from parakeets. If you're ever feeling lonely, just eat in front of a mirror.

Phil Dunphy

Every beautiful woman

deserves flowers...

cauliflowers.

Phil Dunphy

Older black women make

the best iced tea.

Phil Dunphy

Key to a good birthday?

Low expectations.

Phil Dunphy

You can tell a lot about a

person from his biography.

Phil Dunphy

Success is 1% inspiration,

98% perspiration and 2%

attention to detail.

Phil Dunphy

Watch the sun rise at least

once a day.

Phil Dunphy

If you love something,

set it free.

Unless it's a tiger.

Phil Dunphy

If you're ever making jam,

a crayon scrunched up

under your nose makes a

good pretend moustache.

Phil Dunphy

Sometimes God closes a door.

But sometimes he closes it so

hard you can't get your wife

out.

Phil Dunphy

The most amazing things that

can happen to a human being

will happen to you if you just

lower your expectations.

Phil Dunphy

I was 11 years old.

I hit ten straight fastballs in

the batting cage, then my

friend Jeff Sweeney got one

in the groin.

I yelled "ball two!".

Everybody laughed.

That's when I knew I was

funny.

Phil Dunphy

So dumb guys go for dumb

girls, and smart guys go for dumb
girls. Then what do the

smart girls get?

Cats, mostly.

Phil Dunphy

You don't tell a man on the

throes of a Celine Dion

concert to grow a pair.

The ship sank, but her love

will last forever!

Phil Dunphy

I got to be the top realtor of

the year by thinking inside the

box. That's right, I said inside.

because while everyone is

chasing each other outside,

what is in the box?

(Nobody)

Phil Dunphy

If you show enough houses,
you learn all the tricks. Every
realtor is just a ninja with a
blazer. The average burglar
breaks in and leaves clues
everywhere, but not me.
I'm completely clueless.

Phil Dunphy

On parenting:

Your parents faked their way
through it. You fake your way
through it and just hope you
did not raise a serial killer.

Phil Dunphy

I always felt bad for people
with emotionally distant
fathers. It turns out I'm
one of them. It's a miracle I
did not end up a stripper.

Phil Dunphy

I'm a cool dad, that's my thing. I'm hip, I surf the web, I text.

LOL: Laugh out loud
OMG: Oh my God!
WTF: Why the face?

Phil Dunphy

Act like a parent, talk

       like a peer.

I call it "peer-renting".

Phil Dunphy

Never be afraid to reach for
the stars, because even if you
fall, you will always be
wearing a "Parentchute".

Phil Dunphy

On marriage:

Marry someone who looks

sexy while disappointed.

Phil Dunphy

You can kiss my wife, you can

take her to bed, but you cannot
make her laugh.

I wanna go back.

You can kiss my wife, but only I

can take her to bed and make

her laugh. I wanna go back.

Only I can take her to bed,

comma, and make her laugh.

Phil Dunphy

On fear:

I am brave. Roller coasters?

Love 'em. Scary movies? I've seen

   Ghostbusters like 7 times.

   I regularly drive through

neighborhoods that have only

recently been gentrified. So yeah

  I am pretty much not afraid of

        anything.

Phil Dunphy

I wish I was one of those people
who thrived on the dangers of
living a double life.

Bruce Wayne, Peter Parker,
Hannah Montana.

Phil Dunphy

On alcohol:

What is Jagermeister?
You know how in a fairy tale there's
always a potion that makes the
Princess fall asleep and then the guy
starts kissing her?
Well, this is like that, except you
don't wake up in a castle-you
wake up in a frat house with a bad
reputation.

Phil Dunphy

If life gives you lemonade-make lemons and life will be like "Whaaaat?"

Phil Dunphy

It's gonna be tough to say goodbye, it always is. Nobody loves change, but, part of life is learning to let things go.

And remember, if you ever are in a situation, and don't know what to do, just think WWPDD. (What would Phil Dunphy do?)

Phil Dunphy

Extra Inspirational Quotes...

"Whatever you do,

always give 100%.

 Unless you're

Donating blood."

Bill Murray

There are two rules

for success:

1. Never reveal everything

you know.

2.

Roger H. Lincoln

"You can't have everything. Where would you put it?"

Steven Wright

I dedicate this book to anyone who
made me laugh or smile.

Rachel Paniccia

The End

Made in United States
Orlando, FL
18 December 2022

27019882R00046